What Our Readers Have Said...

Applicability

"These books are great tools that should be used as guidelines for our everyday supervisory practices. You need to take the time to do a short self-evaluation when reading them."

•

"The things and problems we deal with everyday are discussed in these books."

•

Convenience

"I like this because I can take them with me to read at a convenient time. I feel the little time I have to spend in the office is best use on activities that directly relate to revenue opportunities. I like the short amount of time it takes to keep up with these."

•

"I just read each book, and then file it for future reference."

•

"I like the fact that the format allows the books to be reviewed as time permits. All work has been conducted on personal, evening/weekend time."

•

Challenge

"My thought is that the real value of these books comes into effect when doing the action plans."

•

"The challenge when I think a specific topic does not apply is to find a way to make it apply."

•

Clarity

"Short and sweet. These books are easy to comprehend."

•

"These books are very easy to read and clearly outlined."

•

"Easy to use, understand, and reference if needed."

•

Relevance

"I have enjoyed reading these books. They are relevant to today's work environment and the ongoing change in the way we manage our workforce."

•

"I believe the contents of the Pinpoint series are excellent. It causes one to reflect on the daily dynamics in working with oneself as well as with management and peers."

•

"I do feel that these books have been very helpful to me at my job."

•

"I do enjoy reading each of theses books and it gives some real thought to its instruction."

•

Identifying & Meeting Customer Expectations

Pinpoint Customer Service Skill Development Training Series

TIMOTHY F. BEDNARZ

BUSINESS PRESS

Pinpoint Customer Service Skill Development Training Series
"Identifying & Meeting Customer Expectations"
Timothy F. Bednarz

Graphic design: Monika Pawlak

Majorium Business Press
2025 Main Street
Stevens Point, WI 54481
715.342.1018 • 800.654.4935

Copyright © 2011 Timothy F. Bednarz, Ph.D. All rights reserved. No part of this publication may be reproduced, distributed or transmitted in any form or by any means, including photocopying, recording, or other electronic or mechanical methods, without author's written permission.

ISBN 978-1-882181-28-5

Printed in the United States of America

Introduction

The Pinpoint Customer Service Skill Development Training Series is designed for targeted training and education regarding increased improvement in a specific skill or competency.

Each book within this series is designed to be easy to use, understand and apply to your job. It can be used as a basis for training individuals, as a discussion guide or as a personal training tool.

Each chapter within this book discusses a specific concept. When you have completed all eight chapters you should have a 360º perspective of the topic.

Additionally, each chapter is divided into specific sections:

- The first section provides you with an overview of the topic
- The Implications section discusses why the concept is important, and why it is important to learn and apply.
- The Strategies, Tips & Techniques to Apply section teaches how to use and apply the particular concept to your work.
- The Points to Ponder section gives you something to think about or to be discussed with a group setting. These are questions not meant to be immediately answered, but to be pondered over time.
- The Training Activity section provides you with the tools to transfer what you have learned to your job. It is designed to help create an action plan to effectively apply the concept.

Each of the topics in this series is time-tested and proven in the marketplace. They have been used by thousands of employees as training tools. Many of the users have commented that what made these books valuable, was the ability to refer to them when a problem surfaced. They indicated that they remembered reading about the exact problem. They referred back to these books and found an appropriate solution.

You will find them equally valuable as a resource in your professional development library.

Table of Contents

1. Understanding the Power of Perception 1

2. How Perceptions Shape Expectations 5

3. Expectations Do Define Value in the Customer's Mind 9

4. When Representatives Fail to Manage Their Customer's Perceptions and Expectations 13

5. The Customer's Moments of Truth 17

6. Managing Your Moments of Truth 21

7. Managing Customer's Perceptions and Expectations 25

8. Controlling Perceptions 29

LEARNING OBJECTIVES:

- The role of perception and expectations in customer service.
- How to identify customer expectations.
- How to manage customer expectations.
- How to meet and exceed customer expectations.
- How to define and deliver value to the customer.
- How to assure customer satisfaction.

1

Understanding the Power of Perception

One of the most powerful yet least understood tools a customer service representative has at his or her disposal is the power to create, shape and control a customer's perceptions. This is done through the sum total of statements made to customers and the actual words and language used. The customer then mentally forms expectations based upon these perceptions.

It is dangerous to ignore or misuse the power of perception. Unfortunately, most service representatives are unaware this tool exits, or if they are, so grossly misapply it that they do more to damage than grow the account.

IMPLICATIONS — WHAT THIS MEANS TO YOU

Every customer has ideas and expectations of what constitutes good service. Salespeople, advertising, the company's image and a host of other factors create these expectations. These perceptions and expectations often remain unspoken or hidden throughout the sale and even during the actual delivery and use of a product or service. A service representative can deliver each of the specific items ordered by a customer only to be told it was not what they expected. Rather than developing a positive customer relationship through the delivery of value, the company is wasting valuable time and resources in damage-control mode. The burden is now on the representative to backtrack in order to satisfy the previously uncommunicated—and, in fact, often unrealistic—expectations created in the sales process.

STRATEGIES, TIPS & TECHNIQUES TO APPLY

Perceptions are created in a number of ways. Many are established in previous experiences with salespeople and their company or through interaction with competitors. Customers may form preconceived notions based upon the name and reputation of a company, its advertising, promotional materials, web site or prior customer use. Once formed, perceptions and especially preconceived notions are difficult to displace. Yet they can represent an extremely powerful and beneficial impetus for results if properly formed and acted upon.

Initial interactions between salespeople and a prospect or customer create specific perceptions that can color the entire relationship. This is why it is important for salespeople to develop a consistent professional attitude and image in everything they say, think and do. Often salespeople's behaviors, statements and promises create problems for the company after the sale has been closed and they have exited from the picture. These then can be the seed for future problems they must resolve.

Salespeople have the power to shape and craft positive and realistic perceptions through their words, tone and semantics as well as their use of sales tools, product demonstrations and sales presentations. The images and ideas they create all contribute to whether positive or negative perceptions are created. This is why the use of unsubstantiated and undocumented claims about a product's performance can ultimately undermine the entire effort. While this might be acceptable for people looking for a quick sale, it is highly detrimental to the pursuit of stress-free, long-term relationships.

Additionally, salespeople can undermine the entire effort by creating conflicting perceptions. For instance, if the prospect or customer has already developed a certain perception based on the company's advertising or image, and the sales person fails to meet these expectations, this creates an immediate problem. Salespeople also can create mixed messages with a general misuse or lack of appreciation for the power of perceptions. When this occurs, sales and service representatives often have no idea why sale efforts and relationships literally collapse before them.

Salespeople and other company representatives take meticulous care in crafting positive perceptions when they deal with a prospect or customer. They pay close attention when relating thoughts, concepts, and ideas, and choose their tone and words with an eye towards conveying a consistently positive message. When properly done, service representatives will experience fewer problems and increased customer satisfaction.

POINTS TO PONDER — SOMETHING TO THINK ABOUT

1. What impact do the perceptions you create have on your overall success with customers?
2. Have you ever lost a customer for no apparent reason? Thinking back on it, could it have been due to the perceptions and expectations you created?

TRAINING ACTIVITY — APPLICATION & ACTION PLAN

On a sheet of paper, list the concepts, phrases, words and images that you use to service your customers. Next to each, determine the perception created.
1. Determine if each creates either a positive or negative perception.
2. Determine if the perceptions are consistent with one another.
3. Identify ways to improve and sharpen the perceptions you create.

2

How Perceptions Shape Expectations

During the course of daily activities, every single person develops perceptions about their world and the people they encounter. Every human sense is involved in the process and judgments made based upon the information collected. This is done unconsciously and without regard to pertinent objective factors that would otherwise put assumptions in a different light.

Everything absorbed and experienced by a customer creates a perception. Many have impressions of a company and its products prior to a direct contact with a representative. The fact that these perceptions are formed involuntarily can be used to the sales representative's advantage: through careful crafting of perceptions, powerful positive impressions can easily be created in the customer's mind.

IMPLICATIONS — WHAT THIS MEANS TO YOU

Individual perceptions and judgments are seldom verbalized, yet they are real and can immediately taint a relationship. Service representatives not only shape but also increase the number of perceptions created in the customer's mind. If this is not understood and controlled, they can undermine their activities by creating poor or unrealistic perceptions. The customer always translates the sum total of perceptions into a set of expectations.

■ STRATEGIES, TIPS & TECHNIQUES TO APPLY

Most customer perceptions have been created by the sales, advertising, promotion and marketing efforts of a company. Additionally, positive or negative news or events create corresponding impressions. It is important for service representatives to be aware of these external sources of input a customer is continually exposed to. When a company invests time and capital in creating a strong and positive image, service representatives should build on this with the perceptions and expectations they themselves create.

All of these efforts to build a consistent and positive image in the customer's mind create expectations of the quality of the product/service, the results they should receive from their investment, and the level of customer service they will receive after the sale. If these expectations are not met, service representatives will find a positive relationship difficult or impossible to achieve.

One of the pitfalls many customer service reps fall into is failing to understand the power and impact that created perceptions have on a customer. When they are careless with their words and the images they convey, this leads to ideas and messages being miscommunicated—and the unnecessary creation of unrealistic expectations and problems.

In other cases salespeople take a lackadaisical approach to selling, using the same presentation for large and small customers alike. A problem arises in that the same perceptions and expectations are created, but in the case of the smaller customer it may be impractical to provide the same level of service that can be provided to larger and more profitable accounts. When smaller customers then inevitably fail to get their expected level of service, they are dissatisfied. This problem typically falls right into the service rep's lap and is difficult, if not impossible, to resolve to the customer's satisfaction.

Additionally, customers have an idea of the treatment and level of service they ought to receive. Service representatives with negative or uncaring attitudes will clash with these expectations. This results in additionally difficult and needless problems. Research has demonstrated that one poor experience in which expectations are left unmet can destroy the company's entire investment in cultivating a positive relationship with that customer.

It is important for service representatives to understand their customer's perceptions and expectations of the service they receive. Careful questioning can identify these factors and help them take the steps needed to meet and exceed these expectations.

> **POINTS TO PONDER — SOMETHING TO THINK ABOUT**
>
> 1. What has been your experience with customers who, based on their experiences, have created unrealistic expectations before you had an opportunity to service them?
> 2. How successful have you been in altering or changing a customer's faulty and unrealistic perceptions?

TRAINING ACTIVITY — APPLICATION & ACTION PLAN

Conduct a review of your company's advertising, promotional and sales materials.

1. Determine the kind of message each conveys.
2. Identify the consistent sales and marketing message created by your company.
3. Examine your own service approach, message and presentation.
4. Determine if it is consistent with the sales and marketing message conveyed by your company.
5. Identify the personal perceptions you create and what you need to do to ensure your efforts send a message that is consistent with your company's mission and image.

3

Expectations Do Define Value in the Customer's Mind

It is not uncommon for customers to complain to a service representative by specifically voicing displeasure with an order received. The service representative carefully goes down the purchase order identifying the exact items the customer ordered and how each meets his or her specifications, only to hear, "It's not what I expected," or "The product or service doesn't perform up to my expectations." In both cases a situation has been created that is difficult to rectify.

Customers repeatedly indicate that they are seeking value in the products and services they want to purchase or have purchased. Many confuse value with the lowest cost available. The real definition of value is "a company's ability to repeatedly meet and exceed the customer's expectations in a host of areas including price, service and quality."

IMPLICATIONS — WHAT THIS MEANS TO YOU

The true definition of value highlights why the study of perceptions and the expectations they create is so vital to customer service representatives. As companies are increasingly seeking to build quality customer relationships and improve retention, the consistent delivery of value takes on a heightened significance. When customer service representatives understand and master the concept of creating positive perceptions, they are able to manage the customer's expectations of the value he or she will receive. This helps assure that value is consistently delivered over the long-term.

Service representatives failing to develop this critical skill will not be in tune with expectations and risk being blindsided by unhappy clients.

STRATEGIES, TIPS & TECHNIQUES TO APPLY

When service representatives are surprised by an unhappy customer's response to what appears to be a perfectly executed order, they are baffled as to why a problem arose. Most are left guessing as to what transpired to bring the situation about. These undesirable circumstances are usually created by two primary factors: faulty perceptions and undefined or unrealistic expectations. Both are manageable and under the direct control of both the sales and customer service representative.

If a problem exists, care must be taken to examine root causes. In most instances, it will likely not be a problem with the product itself, but one directly linked to the customer's expectations of what it would accomplish and the letdown when it didn't deliver.

Individuals make buying decisions with specific expectations of what a product will deliver. These may have been created through advertising, experiences passed along from others or from their own personal impressions. Expectations can include improving efficiency, reducing operating expenses and increasing profitability. Other reasons may be more closely related to personal factors such as pride, ego and greed.

Often before the actual contact, customers have already formed expectations. Whether reasonable or unrealistic, these can form the basis of the sale. If left unmodified, these expectations will prove a weak foundation upon which to build the relationship. They are the seeds of potential problems that will germinate after the sale, when it is more often than not difficult, if not too late, for the company to recover.

Customer service representatives must take care to avoid creating faulty perceptions during the service process. This only complicates an existing problem. Problems are often the consequence of an unmanaged sales approach, where rash and unrealistic claims and statements were made. Unlike anywhere else, the customer will hold the company accountable for what is said during the sales process. An order might be gained by the use of these tactics, but the business relationship and subsequent sales may be lost. Often the salesperson has entirely left the picture, leaving customer service representatives to pick up the pieces and fix the problem. Therefore, it is important for service representatives to carefully manage the perceptions and expectations they create.

Customer service representatives must understand that the words and tone they use, as well as the specific images they create and their personal attitude toward the customer, are foundational to their ability to shape a situation's outcome.

While most customers accept the fact that problems will occur, they have little patience for a slow or drawn-out solution. What they want and expect is a fast and acceptable answer that minimizes their inconvenience. Problems arise when customer service representatives take on a surly or defensive position or choose to hide behind company policies. This creates a perception that the company is uncaring and that the customer's business is unimportant. While internal policies may be relevant to the company and its service representatives, they serve only to irritate the customer – sometimes to the point where they will become activists willing to do everything in their power to harm the company and its reputation.

> ### POINTS TO PONDER — SOMETHING TO THINK ABOUT
>
> 1. Have you ever been blindsided by an unhappy customer who felt his or her expectations were not met?
> 2. How aware are you of a customer's expectations from the onset of the contact?

TRAINING ACTIVITY — APPLICATION & ACTION PLAN

Identify the expectations of a customer you are currently working with according to the following criteria:
- The customer's expectations during the delivery, installation and implementation phases.
- The level of productivity and results the customer expects to receive once your product/service is operational.
- The overall results the customer expects to realize and how fast he or she expects to see them.

Determine what actions you need to take to correct any erroneous or unrealistic expectations the customer might have.

When Representatives Fail to Manage Their Customer's Perceptions and Expectations

Few service representatives understand the power they possess in shaping the perceptions and expectations of their customers. Curiously, it is a topic seldom treated in customer service programs or training materials. When service representatives understand and manage perceptions, they create the underlying expectations that buttress any customer relationship. The impact on the delivery of customer satisfaction is enormous.

When service representatives fail to understand the impact of the perceptions they create and the customer's expectations, compound problems occur, often leaving them unsure as to what is actually happening or what to do.

The impact of uncontrolled perceptions and expectations on the customer can be profound. If service representatives are perceptive, they will quickly learn from the adverse consequences of the words they use and images they create. The alternative is to suffer a series of negative events that will be difficult to resolve, let alone understand.

Any customer's outlook is influenced by previous experiences they had with other companies. If their service experiences were positive, they enter into the relationship anticipating a positive experience; if negative they will expect a similarly negative experience.

■ IMPLICATIONS — WHAT THIS MEANS TO YOU

Service representatives hold the power to make or break the customer relationship with their words, attitude, demeanor and actions. Often it only takes a little extra effort to be a service star than to perform at the average level. The impact on the company and the customers can be enormous.

■ STRATEGIES, TIPS & TECHNIQUES TO APPLY

When customers contact a service department, they typically have a problem or question. The product or service has failed to perform to their expectations, technical problems have arisen, or they are seeking information. In all cases they expect a prompt response or resolution. Research bears out that companies responding quickly and positively develop a base of loyal customers. Even hostile and angry customers can be won over with exceptional service.

Simply stated, problems arise when customers don't get what they expect. Some of the following issues directly related to customer satisfaction are problematic for many companies:

Speed and Time

Once the customer has invested their money in a product or service, many companies fail to provide service that respects the customer's time. The fact that a paying customer has a problem and must take the time to solve it is not accounted for. Instead, they are all too often made to feel a bother and inconvenience. There is more focus on internal efficiency and productivity than on the customer who pays the bills and salaries.

Nothing is more annoying to a customer with a problem or question than to have to search around for an answer. This is the crux of most customer service issues. The company and its customer service representatives don't value the customer's time or consider the inconvenience *they* are experiencing. When customers do finally get to speak to a representative, they are in many cases – already and understandably – highly irritated by the hoops they are made to jump through to get assistance.

Further, once the customer has made contact with a service representative, the urgency he or she expresses about his or her problem is minimized or ignored altogether. The representative conveys an attitude that the client is lucky enough to be talking with someone who is supposed to help them (along with a long list of other people with problems), and that should be good enough. It should come as no surprise that this further and deeply irritates them. It *is* surprising how many companies' customer service policies completely undermine their designed purpose. When a customer has a problem or question, they want an *immediate* solution or answer—not to be told that they'll be called in a day or so.

Importance

Customers calling with a problem expect to be made to feel they're important to the company. They spent money on a product or service, and when an issue arises they want to know they and their business are *valued*—not someone the company could easily take or leave. Representatives should constantly think of how they themselves would wish to be treated when calling with a problem. Is the service they are giving what they would want to receive?

Representatives who treat customers poorly, and convey an attitude that they really don't care much about their problems, are literally destroying their company's business. While it is easy to treat customers as "just another problem," this attitude does not help the customer; it alienates them. After the call is completed, the effects are exceptionally long-lasting. In more extreme instances, poorly executed customer service can ultimately escalate into a lawsuit. The costs to a company can be staggering—and could have been completely avoided if its people had treated customers with respect.

Lack of Adherence to External Standards

In many companies, customer satisfaction is measured by internal rather than external standards. The service representative is going to determine when the problem is resolved and the case closed, not the customer. In many instances the customer feels shortchanged by the solution and without any recourse or alternative: they have used up their allotment of assistance. If the problem is large enough, his or her only alternative is to consult an attorney. There is only one person qualified to gauge whether a problem has been adequately addressed: the customer.

Hiding Behind Company Policy

Some service representatives are very accommodating and will move mountains to solve a customer's problems. Others hide behind procedures and policies. Both can work in the same company, but the latter has the idea he or she can use internal policies to minimize their work. Service representatives who rigidly hide behind company policies will face an increasingly angry and hostile population of customers. The last possible thing customers want to hear is, "It's not our policy." Surveys have shown that when customers are offered the opportunity to present their own solutions, they are often more than what the company is prepared to offer. When within reason, companies should be willing to meet the customer's idea of how the problem should be resolved because an investment in retaining an account is an investment in long-term business.

POINTS TO PONDER — SOMETHING TO THINK ABOUT

1. Have you been trapped by your words, demeanor and actions, creating a difficult customer situation?
2. Are you careful about the claims and statements you make to your customer?

TRAINING ACTIVITY — APPLICATION & ACTION PLAN

Identify on a sheet of paper how you present yourself to customers. Gauge yourself according to the following factors:
- Attitude
- Demeanor
- Words
- Concern
- Flexibility
- Compassion

5

The Customer's Moments of Truth

It is the response to customers' expectations and problems that determines whether they are satisfied or unhappy, ecstatic or angry. A company or representative's response to concerns determines whether a customer will remain in the relationship or leave for a more responsive vendor.

Every time a service representative has a contact with a customer, they are creating a "moment of truth" for the company. This is the case whether a salesperson, customer service representative, the shipping clerk, delivery person or person answering the phone makes the contact. Each has the power to positively or negatively impact the customer's experience.

IMPLICATIONS — WHAT THIS MEANS TO YOU

This is important for customer service representatives to appreciate because aside from the salesperson handling the customer's account, the customer service representative will have the most contact with the customer. Their attitude, personal demeanor, tone of voice and helpfulness will impact the customer's moment of truth. This is a critical aspect of customer service that all representatives must both understand and apply. Unmanaged moments of truth will result in increased problems, more hostile and angry customers, and lost business.

STRATEGIES, TIPS & TECHNIQUES TO APPLY

The objective of the service representative and the company as a whole is to understand and continuously improve customers' moments of truth. The concept of moments of truth was developed by Scandinavian Airlines as a method of gauging their performance with customers and is a very helpful concept for service representatives to understand.

What Is a Moment of Truth?

Every interaction between a prospect or customer and a company is a moment of truth. Customers have specific expectations of how things should work or how they should be treated. These are the customer's expectations—not the company's or the representative's. Each customer contact provides the service representative and his or her company with an opportunity to meet or exceed the customer's expectations.

While every prospect or customer contact is a moment of truth, there are six critical moments of truth that service representatives should be especially aware of. These are:
- At the time of the sale
- At the time of delivery
- When there is a problem
- When the customer complains
- When the customer is facing competitive pressures
- During follow up calls to retain the business

The Correlation between Customer Fears and Moments of Truth

When identifying customer fears, it is exactly in these six moments of truth most feel companies fail them. When service representatives understand the correlation and know the critical moments of truth in the customer relationship, they can use this information to their advantage. By continuously exceeding his or her prospect or customer's expectations, the service representative is continually adding value to the product or service. This provides service representatives with a real opportunity to shine and create competitive immunity for their company.

What Needs to Be Done

Since every contact provides service representatives with an opportunity to meet or exceed the prospect's or customer's expectations, it is important they clearly identify specific expectations for each critical moment of truth before it occurs.

Additionally, service representatives must identify other critical moments of truth that are important to their prospects or customers. Once identified, they must ask them to relate their specific expectations at each of their critical moments of truth. Without identification of these expectations, it will be difficult for service representatives to satisfy the customer. Long-term relationships are enhanced not by meeting expectations, but by exceeding them. Service representatives must remember this defines value-added service and ensures sustained customer satisfaction.

POINTS TO PONDER — SOMETHING TO THINK ABOUT

1. How cognizant of the concept of identifying moments of truth have you been in the past?
2. What has been your experience when you have failed to handle any one of these critical moments of truth properly? Give an example.

TRAINING ACTIVITY — APPLICATION & ACTION PLAN

Identify a customer or prospect that you consider a typical or average representation of your contacts.
1. Define this typical customer's key moments of truth.
2. Define what makes them critical moments in your relationship.
3. Identify an additional situation when you have lost a customer by failing to meet their expectations.

4. Upon reflection, can you identify the critical moments of truth you may have overlooked? Explain.

6

Managing Your Moments of Truth

In the 1980s Jan Carlson rebuilt Scandinavian Airlines on the concept of "moments of truth." Each second of time that service representative or his or her company has in direct contact with a customer is classified as a moment of truth. A great moment can build a quality relationship, while a bad moment can instantly destroy a relationship that has taken immense time and effort to develop.

The Walt Disney Company created a science of managed moments of truth. At their amusement parks, all employees are considered actors rather than simply workers with duties. Employees are constantly either "on stage" when they enter areas requiring face-to-face contact with customers, or "off stage" when they are in areas off-limits to customers. On stage they are expected to exhibit a professional personality that is helpful, informative and pleasant. This ensures customers always have a pleasant experience—and creates an extremely favorable reputation and corporate image.

IMPLICATIONS — WHAT THIS MEANS TO YOU

Every time service representatives make contact with their customers they must project a professional on stage personality that is pleasant, accommodating and helpful. When customer service representatives assume this professional role, they can successfully manage their customer's experience. This is their primary role and responsibility.

■ STRATEGIES, TIPS & TECHNIQUES TO APPLY

Whether they realize it or not, when service representatives have any customer contact, in any form, they are on stage and projecting an image. A single inattentive moment can instantly undermine or destroy a carefully cultivated customer relationship.

Service representatives clearly cannot control all actions of others within their company who have contact with their customers. They can, however, pay close attention to how their customers are being treated and take immediate corrective action when problems arise to assure they do not occur again. This is managing their customers' moments of truth.

Customers know problems will occur. Each has an expectation of how the company should act, how the product should perform and how he or she is to be treated. While they know problems will arise, they expect service representatives to respond to and correct them immediately. This is how the customer ultimately evaluates his or her experience with the company, and how the future of the relationship is determined.

Managed moments of truth can be defined by three primary attributes. All other actions and activities stem from these three traits. Service representatives with the ability to professionally master and project these assets will be successful in building and maintaining productive relationships with their customers.

Helpful

The principal reason customers contact a company is to have a need met or problem solved. They want help in a way that immediately reduces their stress, and it is the service representative's responsibility to provide it.

The role of the service representative in this context is to facilitate the customer's experience by removing hindrances and obstacles that prevent timely and efficient resolution of their problem. Most service failures occur when these impediments are not removed, or representatives create their own barriers with the inappropriate application of company policies, regulations and rules. When the customer's moments of truth are inadequately managed, at best, the relationship does not progress.

Informative

Service representatives are information resources for the customer. They have the ability to share or withhold information the customer needs or could use. This information can take the form of telling the customer how long a problem will take to resolve, when a product or service will be delivered or additional available options and features.

Service representatives should be as informative as possible. This means volunteering and sharing information with the customer. Often, customers are unaware of the information and options that are available to them. Since they do not know what may be available to them, they are unable to ask for it. It is the role and responsibility of the service representative to provide this level of assistance.

Pleasant

Service representatives must be on stage with their customers at all times. This means creating a professional personality independent of their personal feelings and emotions.

One element of a professional personality is the representative's tone, which should be cheerful and upbeat. Service representatives should further assume a service attitude that clearly conveys they are there to serve the customer and be helpful, courteous and respectful at all times.

POINTS TO PONDER — SOMETHING TO THINK ABOUT

1. Do you allow your personal feelings and emotions to affect how you handle your customers?
2. Do you consider yourself on stage when dealing with a customer?

TRAINING ACTIVITY — APPLICATION & ACTION PLAN

Customers have specific expectations of how they should be treated, including service representatives being helpful, informative and pleasant.

1. List three things you are doing well and three things you are doing poorly under each of these traits.
2. Determine how you can expand upon the things you are doing well and eliminate the things you are doing poorly.
3. Create a personal plan to improve your professional performance.

7

Managing Customer's Perceptions and Expectations

Any customer comes to a company with fundamental expectations of how they should be treated. Surprisingly, many companies are unable to meet these basic requirements. Successful practitioners of customer service recognize these expectations and train their employees to carefully manage and meet them.

Exceptional customer service is delivered when the customer's needs and expectations are thoroughly identified and met. Most service problems stem from the failure to immediately meet basic customer expectations and deal with them in a professional and respectful manner.

IMPLICATIONS — WHAT THIS MEANS TO YOU

Service representatives hold the power to build solid customer relationships and deliver value to sustain the relationship over time. Research has demonstrated that positive customer service experiences can transform a hostile and angry customer into a fiercely loyal advocate of the company.

STRATEGIES, TIPS & TECHNIQUES TO APPLY

In the preceding lessons the concept of "moments of truth," or any contact a company representative has with a customer, was discussed.

A positive moment is achieved when the customer's expectations of the experience were either met or exceeded. A company can deliver sustained value to its customers by consistently meeting or exceeding their expectations. To understand this, it is important to examine basic customer expectations and how customer service representatives can manage them.

Customer Expectations

In virtually any environment, there are four basic expectations a customer has when they deal with a company. These expectations are the foundation of solid customer service, yet many companies fall significantly short of meeting them.

- Customers expect to be treated with courtesy and respect.
- Customers expect to be made to feel their business is valued.
- Customers want their problem solved and solved quickly.
- Customers want prompt and complete answers to their questions.

Few people would characterize these requirements as excessive or unreasonable, and, in fact, most customers are not demanding until these basic expectations are not met. In the majority of these cases, surveys show customers quietly go away without complaint and take their business elsewhere.

Consistency

Service representatives must display a consistency that mirrors their company's image and reputation, while meeting or exceeding their customers' expectations. This consistency must be displayed in their "on stage" behavior with their customers and incorporates the following elements:

Message – Whether service representatives realize it or not, they are communicating a message to the customer with everything they say or do. The message is either, "You are important and I care about your problem," or "I don't care about your problem and would rather you go away."

Service representatives can do everything "by the book" and still communicate an "I would rather you go away" message through the intricacies of verbal and nonverbal communication. Any negative message, no matter how subtle, is clearly conveyed to and received by the customer.

Words and Actions – Service representatives must be consistent in their words and actions. Customers will immediately identify any inconsistencies, and form the opinion that the service representative is both insincere and uncaring. Once this perception is created, everything else the service representative attempts to do will be undermined.

Behaviors – Professional and appropriate service behaviors must be displayed at all times. By the very definition, customer service representatives are there to serve and be of service. Yet, many ignore this concept altogether, bringing their personal problems and issues to the workplace and treating the customer with disrespect and even contempt. While customers' problems may seem minor and insignificant, by purchasing the company's product or service they have earned the right to be served with respect. They pay the bills—and if put off will vote for better service with their feet.

Solutions – Customers' service expectations are proportional to the price they paid for a product or service and the size of their order. In all instances, customers expect a timely and convenient solution to their problems. Surveys show that customers are quite tolerant of problems and product failures—if they are remedied quickly. When they experience poor service, they are far more likely to take their business elsewhere.

Attitudes – Customers expect to deal with service representatives who are cheery, pleasant, helpful and informative regardless of when they call or whom they speak with. This is why the concept of moments of truth and its successful practice is foundational to the success of any company.

POINTS TO PONDER — SOMETHING TO THINK ABOUT

1. Do you recognize the message you communicate to your customers in your words and actions?
2. Do you monitor your service behaviors for consistency during the entire course of the customer relationship to prevent miscommunications and misunderstandings?

TRAINING ACTIVITY — APPLICATION & ACTION PLAN

Examine your personal service behavior to determine if you are consistent in meeting the basic customer expectations discussed:
- Message
- Words and Actions
- Behaviors
- Solutions
- Attitudes

Identify any problem areas and determine what you need to do to correct them.

8

Controlling Perceptions

A customer is only interested in how their problem will be fixed, and service representatives are there to answer his or her questions. During the service process, representatives are painting a picture of how a specific issue will be resolved.

Through service representatives' words, statements and images, perceptions and expectations of the level of service the customer can expect to receive are created. They have the power to paint an accurate picture, or they can greatly exaggerate the levels of service that will be delivered. The service representative decides which version to present and the expectations they will create.

The controlling of customer perceptions takes personal discipline. Service representatives often get into trouble when they are careless with the claims they make. It is often easier to do this and manipulate a customer into a quick sale and allow someone else to worry about any problems that surface later on. This misses the point of developing trust and building future customer relationships.

■ IMPLICATIONS — WHAT THIS MEANS TO YOU

If service representatives make the effort to create precise statements and images, they will eliminate the vast amount of time and energy required to resolve problems stemming from unmet customer expectations. In other words, with a little discipline, value can be ensured and customer satisfaction guaranteed. This is all well within the control of the service representative.

STRATEGIES, TIPS & TECHNIQUES TO APPLY

Service representatives can carefully control the perceptions and expectations they create by closely monitoring the following areas:

Know the Limitations of the Product or Service

Service representatives must fully understand the limitations of their company, products and services. They must know which levels of service are economically and profitably deliverable for which customers. Additionally, they must have product expertise and, as each has specific limitations, be well-versed in the particular capabilities of their products and services. Service representatives must take care not to give customers the idea that a product will deliver more than it is capable of or that the company will provide levels of service beyond what is reasonable and profitable to deliver.

Tailor the Message to the Customer

Service representatives must make a habit of tailoring their message to the customer's specific requirements. This means they must first identify the specific needs of the customer. It also means making sure that the message is crafted so that the specific capabilities of the company and the product or service are conveyed clearly, to preclude the customer from misunderstanding what they can reasonably expect to receive.

Carefully Craft Statements and Images

Exaggerated promises are directly linked to a customer's unrealistic expectations and give rise to multiple problems.

Service representatives must carefully choose their words and closely monitor the statements they make and images they create. Each paints a specific picture in the customer's mind as to what he or she will receive as a return on investment. Each claim must be documentable. If it cannot be, it should not be made.

Service representatives must further use concrete terms and statements and avoid the use of general and purposely vague claims regarding their product or service. This clarity leaves little doubt in the customer's mind as to what they can realistically expect to receive.

Assume Nothing

Many service representatives assume the customer possesses their own level of knowledge and expertise and is familiar with all of the specifications and intricacies of their product and service. In reality, the customer often does not have anywhere near the same level of product awareness as the service representative. This is why they have initiated or agreed to a contact: they are relying on the service representative to provide them the information they can use to resolve their problem or answer their question.

Many service problems stem from these assumptions and the accompanying expectations. Service representatives must be careful that everything is completely laid out with nothing assumed or left to chance.

POINTS TO PONDER — SOMETHING TO THINK ABOUT

1. Do you understand that you have the power to create and manage a customer's perceptions and expectations?
2. Have there been times when you have possibly created faulty perceptions and expectations? Explain.

TRAINING ACTIVITY — APPLICATION & ACTION PLAN

Make a list of words, statements, concepts and images that you typically use in your service activities.
1. Next to each determine the image and perception that each creates.
2. Examine the list of images you create and determine if the images are consistent with each other.

3. Determine if the images you are creating are accurate.
4. Identify other words, statements and images that you can use to reinforce your service message.

About the Author

Timothy F. Bednarz, Ph.D. is CEO of the American Management Development Group, Inc. For over 20 years he has researched, designed and authored hundreds of learning and development programs used by Fortune 1000 companies.

He is also the author of *Great! What Makes Leaders Great. What They Did, How They Did It and What You Can Learn from It* (2011).

Speaking Availability

Timothy F. Bednarz, Ph.D. is available for speaking engagements for your next meeting or association event. He can be contacted at 800-654-4935 or by e-mail at timothy.bednarz@majorium.com.

Bulk Sales

Bulk sales of this book or any other titles available from Majorium Business Press. Inquiries can be directed to sales@majorium.com, or by phone at 800-6654-4935.

Quick Order Form

Fax orders: 715-342-1118. Send this form.

Telephone orders: Call 800-654-4935 toll-free. Have your credit card ready.

Email orders: sales@majorium.com

Postal orders: Majorium Business Press, 2025 Main Street, Stevens Point, WI 54481, USA.

Please send the following books:

_____

_____

_____

_____

Please send more FREE information on:

❏ Catalog   ❏ Speaking/Seminars   ❏ Mailing Lists   ❏ Consulting

Name: _____

Address: _____

City: _____ State: _____ Zip: _____

Telephone: _____

Email address: _____

Sales tax: Please add 5.5% for products shipped to Wisconsin addresses.

Shipping by air:

United States: $4.00 for first book and $2.00 for each additional product.

International: $9.00 for first book; $5.00 for each additional product (estimate).

Made in the USA
San Bernardino, CA
14 May 2014